50 LGBTQ+ FINDS FROM THE PORTABLE ANTIQUITIES SCHEME

Ben Paites

AMBERLEY

First published 2025

Amberley Publishing
The Hill, Stroud
Gloucestershire, GL5 4EP

www.amberley-books.com

ISBN 978 1 3981 2211 6 (print)
ISBN 978 1 3981 2212 3 (ebook)

British Library Cataloguing in Publication Data.
A catalogue record for this book is available from
the British Library.

Typeset in 10pt on 13pt Celeste.
Typesetting by SJmagic DESIGN SERVICES, India.
Printed in the UK.

Appointed GPSR EU Representative: Easy Access
System Europe Oü, 16879218
Address: Mustamäe tee 50, 10621, Tallinn, Estonia
Contact Details: gpsr.requests@easproject.com,
+358 40 500 3575

Contents

Acknowledgements

I would like to thank the wonderful staff at the Portable Antiquities Scheme who record thousands of objects each year, as well as the members of the public who have shared their finds. Not only do these discoveries help us better understand the complex history of Britain, but they also allow us to tell exciting new stories through those objects.

I would also like to thank Sacha Coward who looked through my first draft. His incredible insight and unparalleled knowledge of all things LGBTQ+, specifically relating to history and folklore, really allowed me to fine-tune the content of this book.

Introduction

This book explores fifty objects, found by members of the public and recorded with the Portable Antiquities Scheme (PAS), that relate to LGBTQ+ history and culture. I consider this to be the history of individuals who did not conform to the expectations of sexuality and gender at the time and within the cultures they lived. Some objects are directly linked

A carnelian intaglio showing Ganymede and Zeus in the form of an eagle, COLEM:2019.31. (Copyright Colchester Museums, image credit Douglas Atfield)

to individuals, while others relate to themes and symbols adopted by or reflected in the LGBTQ+ community. The objects themselves are recorded on the website www.finds.org.uk and can be found by searching their numbers, e.g. WMID-716870.

The book is divided into five chapters. Chapter One focuses on historical figures, exploring the lives of individuals who did not conform to a modern understanding of heterosexuality or whose gender identity has been questioned by historians, themselves or the people who lived alongside them. Although I use modern terminology at times to discuss their identities, it is important to remember that these are not the terms they or their contemporaries would have used.

Chapter Two explores the natural world. It has been well documented that many animals have been observed in same sex activity and can even change biological sex. Animals and plants have also become symbols within the LGBTQ+ community, either relating to individuals or groups of people.

Chapter Three covers language and symbolism. The focus is on the English language and changes in terminology that have occurred throughout history. When language is not a suitable way of communicating, due to fears of 'outing' (don't worry, there's a glossary of terms at the end) or putting people in danger of abuse or even criminal charges, symbols have been used to represent different characteristics or groups within the LGBTQ+ community.

Chapter Four looks at mythology and folklore, with a focus on Roman and Norse myths and British folklore. Although many myths are used to teach morality and social expectations, some can also help us understand attitudes within past societies. Myths from across the world include same-sex relationships and gender non-conforming individuals, often portrayed in a completely normalised way.

The final chapter looks at communities, specifically groups of people that existed throughout history with different attitudes towards sexuality and gender than their contemporaries. Sometimes this was what is described as situational, meaning the rules of society stop applying to these groups due to the situation they are in. This also relates to the creation of safe spaces at times when homosexuality was illegal, to ensure people could live their lives without fear of persecution or even death.

The history of non-heterosexual relationships and people who did not stick to the gender norms of their time is a long and diverse one. The term LGBTQ+ is used to cover a wide range of identities relating to sexuality and gender. The term even goes beyond this to include romantic attraction and individuals who don't identify with any of those characteristics.

One thing that is important to remember when studying the past is that we are limited to the perspectives and terminology of the sources that survive. As discussed later in this book, words like 'gay' to refer to same-sex attraction did not exist until quite recently. This makes it difficult to understand some relationships between historical figures. Words such as 'love' are often used between friends but can still be used in a romantic sense. Many historians have chosen to side with the 'friends' interpretation, meaning that romantic relationships are overlooked. As students of LGBTQ+ history it is important to consider other perspectives, but equally not make that the authoritative answer. It is acceptable to leave some stories open to interpretation, whilst ensuring we don't shut off all perspectives.

A gay rights demonstration at the Democratic National Convention in New York City, photographed by Warren K. Leffler on 11 July 1976. (Image courtesy of The Library of Congress, no: 2005696365)

Chapter 1
Historical Figures

LGBTQ+ people have always existed. In some periods, their stories are more difficult to find than others. For societies without known written language, which in Britain is before the Romans arrived in 43 CE, we must either use sources from other societies to try and understand their attitudes towards sexuality and gender or attempt an interpretation through the objects that have been left behind. As no written sources exist before the Iron Age in Britain, it is almost impossible to explore LGBTQ+ lives at that time.

In Britain, our understanding of life in the Iron Age mostly comes from Roman sources and archaeology. The Romans had a particular view on gender and sexuality themselves, which they of course applied to the people living in Britain. The historian Diodorus Siculus noted that it was perfectly acceptable within Iron Age British society for men to have sexual relationships with other men. In fact, he suggests that the men of Iron Age Britain preferred men to women. However, this may have been an attempt by a Roman writer to portray the people of Britain as subservient, considering the Romans predominantly saw same-sex activity as linked to social status.

Equally, through archaeological discoveries such as the lavish burial at Vix in France, our understanding of gendered objects in the Iron Age has been questioned. Skeletons, even when well preserved, show a range of characteristics that can be used to guess a person's sex. This, in combination with the types of objects found with them, are often used to attempt to identify a person's gender. However, there is a spectrum within both sex and gender and many historians and archaeologists in the past have chosen to try to fit people into a binary of man and woman, rather than consider alternative interpretations.

In later history, writing was primarily an activity of the church. Very few people could write, or even read, and so much of what was produced in medieval Europe was made by monks or the rich and powerful. This, of course, is a very small proportion of society and with their own view on sexuality and gender. Even when we do get some written records that suggest same-sex attraction between people existed, the language used can make it difficult to know the true nature of their relationship. Terms like 'brotherhood' did not always mean 'related by blood' and 'love' between men at court would not always have been platonic.

For most of the people in this chapter, we cannot say for certain what their sexuality or gender was. This is partly because they may never have explicitly shared that information publicly, but also as the terminology we use today did not exist back then. So, in the same way, we can't say for certain that they were straight or cisgendered.

This is a modern silver seal matrix containing a Roman intaglio showing Alexander the Great. An intaglio is a carved stone, often set into rings or other objects, to be pressed into wax as an early form of signature. The spear, cloak and sword shown in this example are often used in depictions of the Macedonian king Alexander.

Alexander the Great was ruler of Macedonia from 336 BCE until his death in 323 BCE. He conquered land from Italy to the area that is now India, through a series of military campaigns and allegiances. He died at the young age of thirty-two. Some accounts suggest he was poisoned as a result of increasing distrust amongst his allies, while others suggest it was an unknown illness.

Through various accounts, Alexander is known to have had relationships with men as well as marrying at least three women. His closest male companion throughout much of his life was Hephaestion, a Macedonian noble. Both made comparisons between themselves and the mythical Achilles and Patroclus, who were also believed to have been lovers. Alexander in fact named Hephaistion φιλαλέξανδρος (Philalexandros), meaning lover of Alexander. However, the word for love chosen in this instance, 'φίλια', is not romantic love but refers more to friendship. Despite this, Alexander's reaction to Hephaistion's death can be seen as an indication that his feelings may have been stronger. The historian Arrian describes how Alexander flung himself onto the body of Hephaestion after his death and cried over him all day, until he was forcefully removed.

The historian Plutarch notes Alexander's openness for affection towards the eunuch Bagoas, describing Alexander kissing them openly in public. Some earlier Babylonian sources refer to eunuchs as separate to men and women, making them a third gender. Equally there were many eunuchs who were castrated to prevent them from producing children within the royal household, suggesting they had little choice in the matter. It is not clear from the sources where Bagoas would have sat in terms of these categories.

Above left: A Roman intaglio of Alexander the Great set into a medieval seal matrix, WMID-716870.

Above right: An engraving showing Hephaestion (on the left), Parmenion and Amyntas. Photograph by Helle Nanny Brendstrup. (© Thorvaldsens Museum – CC0. Accession number: E361)

An engraving of Alexander and Roxana by Giulio Bonasone, 1531–76. (Image courtesy of the Met Museum, Harris Brisbane Dick Fund, 1942. Accession number: 42.128.5)

Alexander also had relationships with others throughout his life. Most notable were his marriages to Roxanna, a princess from the Eurasian Steppes, and Stateira, the daughter of defeated King Darius III. Although you could argue these marriages were political, Alexander also had children with these women. Therefore, we could consider Alexander might not have been exclusively heterosexual. However, it is important to remember that sexuality at this time in Macedonia, and wider Greece, was very different to our modern perspectives.

This is a silver denarius of the Roman emperor Hadrian and a Roman furniture fitting possibly showing the youth Antinous. Hadrian was ruler of the Roman Empire from 117–138 CE. He is well known for having funded many large-scale building projects, such as the eponymous wall and the Pantheon in Rome. Although Hadrian married a woman named Vibia Sabina, this was more of a political allegiance and the pair never had children. It was the young man Antinous who was arguably his greatest love.

Hadrian met Antinous whilst travelling through Greece in the sixth or seventh year of his reign. Antinous was much younger than Hadrian, though we do not know his exact age. Hadrian, a lover of Greek culture and customs, was perhaps trying to copy a practice common in some classical Greek states: the relationship between an older man, known as an 'erastes', and a young man, known as an 'eromenos'. In places like Athens and Sparta, relationships like this were part of the culture. Some have argued this was a wider practice

A silver denarius of the Emperor Hadrian, LIN-263BD3.

A copper-alloy fitting showing the bust of a youth, probably Antinous, ESS-B39770.

11

A cameo of the busts of Hadrian and Antinous carved in sardonyx in a gold setting, possibly a brooch or a pin, dating to the mid-1700s. (Image courtesy of the Met Museum, The Milton Weil Collection, 1939. Accession number: 39.22.41)

of educating young men in subjects such as politics and philosophy, with sex included. However, others have argued that these relationships did in some instances have genuine romantic connections.

Seven years after the pair met, whilst travelling through Egypt, Antinous died in mysterious circumstances. Politicians at the time thought Antinous had too much of an influence over Hadrian, perhaps leading to the young man's murder. Others have argued it was simply an accident. A more radical suggestion is that Hadrian himself killed Antinous, as an offering to the gods. Regardless of the true events, it is clear from the aftermath that Hadrian was devastated. After his death, the emperor set up commemorative shrines across the Empire, built a city and named it after him and turned Antinous into a god.

Deifying Antinous may initially seem to be a true indication of love and affection, however Hadrian also deified his wife. Vibia Sabina is one of very few empresses to be turned into a god after their death. Whether this was because Hadrian actually loved her, or because he believed it was a politically appropriate thing to do, we will never know. From accounts of the relationship while the pair were married, it seems unlikely he did it out of love.

This is a silver finger ring with a denarius of the Emperor Elagabalus set into the bezel. Roman coins were sometimes used as a form of personal adornment once they went out of circulation. Rings of this type could have been worn by people of any gender.

Named Marcus Aurelius Antoninus, he was later called Elagabalus or Heliogabalus after his family connection with the priesthood for the god Elagabal. His short reign as emperor was from 218 to 222 CE. Elagabalus' gender has been a matter of debate amongst historians for many years, often citing sources that say the emperor explicitly asked for female terms to be used when describing them. One example, recounted by the historian Cassius Dio, states that when Elagabalus met a man named Zoticus they asked to be referred to as 'domina', meaning 'mistress' or 'madam'. Another account by Cassius Dio states that Elagabalus offered a lot of money for a doctor who might perform surgery on their genitals so they could have a vagina.

A silver ring with a coin of Elagabalus set into the bezel, DOR-B43092.

The River Tiber in Rome, where the body of Elagabalus was thrown after he was murdered. (Image courtesy of Pexels)

Of course, as with all historical accounts, we must read this within the context of the time and culture it was written. We know many Roman historians used effeminacy to discredit former emperors, so accounts of Elagabalus asking for female-gendered words to be used about them could simply be propaganda. However, there is likely some truth in the claims as historians did not make the same assertions about every emperor. Furthermore, these accounts were made soon after Elagabalus died, meaning the intended readers would have been familiar with the emperor's life and would likely be able to spot any overt lies.

Elagabalus was an emperor that did not behave like other emperors, evoking criticism in contemporary accounts. They questioned their own gender identity and actively presented as both male and female throughout their short life, having been assassinated at the age of eighteen. They never really had the opportunity to live life as their true self.

This is a silver pilgrim badge or button with the image of St Sebastian. It was probably made at some point in the 1400s.

St Sebastian was a member of the Roman Praetorian Guard, protectors of the emperor. He was found to be a Christian during the reign of Diocletian and sentenced to be killed by arrows. Although many believe this was his cause of death, due to the depiction of it in art, the story of Sebastian suggests he lived and was healed by St Irene of Rome. He was later martyred by stoning.

Although there is no real indication that the historical figure of Sebastian had same-sex relationships, his image has been adopted by the gay community in recent years. Perhaps this is because he features in medieval and later art as a symbol of masculine desire, the metaphor of his body being penetrated by many arrows or his presence as a symbol of resisting persecution.

A painting of Sebastian by Guido Reni is used as the backdrop for a same-sex encounter in Yukio Mishima's 1949 novel 仮面の告白 (*Kamen no Kokuhaku – Confessions of a Mask*), showing the extent to which the saint has become a global symbol of same-sex desire.

Above: A silver pilgrim badge showing the martyrdom of St Sebastian, SF-C555E9.

Right: An engraving of St Sebastian by Albrecht Dürer, 1499. (Image courtesy of the Met Museum, gift of Henry Walters, 1917. Accession number: 17.37.111)

This is a brooch made from a coin of William II, who ruled England from 1087–1100 CE. He was the son of William I, often referred to as William the Conqueror, who took control of England in 1066.

When William II became king, he made a lot of changes at court. Rather than employing his father's advisors, it is said that he sought out young and attractive men to fill these roles. One such individual was Ranulf Flambard, who was the bishop of Durham. It was suggested by some at the time and in more recent history that they had a sexual relationship, although there is no strong evidence to prove this. Many of the accusations of homosexuality that came later were from the Church, who were also displeased with William's rule.

Some modern historians have suggested the king may have been bisexual, though again there is limited evidence for his sexual activity with anyone. He never chose a wife or had any legitimate children, which is perhaps more indicative of asexuality or self-imposed chastity.

Left: A silver penny of William II turned into a brooch, HAMP-C95B4.

Below left: An engraving of William II by Renold Elstrack. (Image courtesy of National Portrait Gallery, Smithsonian Institution. Accession number: S/NPG.77.43.3)

William Rufus King of England and Duke of Normandy: He was slaine being shot into the body by misfortune in new Forest in Hampshire, after he had raigned 12 yeares and 11 monthes at the age of 43, and lieth buried at Winchester Anno 1100

This is a medieval gold 'tau' cross, dating to the late 1400s or early 1500s. It may have been a pendant on a necklace, with the suspension loop now missing. This style of cross, similar to the Greek letter 'tau', was adopted as the signature of St Francis of Assisi.

Francis was born in Assisi in 1181 CE, founding the Franciscan order of monks when he was twenty-seven years old. He spent much of his life in poverty, which became one of the three key vows of the Franciscan order, along with chastity and obedience.

Some have speculated about Francis' gender identity, based both on accounts from the time and some of the saintly imagery produced around him. He supposedly had those in his monastic order refer to him as mother, as well as referring to himself as a woman on several occasions. In fact, Francis is one of several saints who resisted gender binaries.

It has also been noted that Francis had a male companion in later life whose name seems to have been lost to history. It may have been Brother Elias of Cortona as several accounts suggest they used affectionate terms for one another and, upon Francis' death, Elias described the saint's body as 'soft and pliable' suggesting they might have had a level of intimacy.

A gold tau cross, SUR-315095.

17

They Shelter in a Cave by José Benlliure y Gil, 1926. It shows Francis of Assisi and a man, possibly his lover. (Image courtesy of Wikimedia Commons)

This is a silver penny of Edward II, who was king of England from 1307–1327 CE. He became king at a challenging time for the British monarchy, due to ongoing conflict with Scotland and France.

Before he became king, Edward was known to have had a very close relationship with a man named Piers Gaveston. The closeness of their relationship was so strongly felt by Edward's father, King Edward I, that the king sent Piers into exile to remove him from his son's presence. Later accounts hinted at a sexual relationship between Edward II and Piers, though this may have been propaganda.

In 1307, after Edward had been crowned king, Gaveston returned from exile to join him at court. Many of the barons were not happy about this and accusations of theft and influence over the king started to circulate. This growing tension culminated in Gaveston being arrested and executed as a traitor.

In 1327 Edward's long-neglected wife Queen Isabella led a rebellion against Edward and he was eventually forced to abdicate, with the promise that his son would only become king if he did so. Although Edward agreed, this would not be the end of his punishment. Edward died at Berkeley Castle, where he had been held as a prisoner for six months. Some say that he had been murdered, with a red-hot poker inserted into his anus as a punishment for his alleged sexuality. However, the true circumstances of his death are unknown.

A silver penny of Edward II, IOW-2C809.

19

Berkeley Castle, 9 August 2009. Edward II was imprisoned and died here. Photograph by Philip Halling. (Image courtesy of Wikimedia Commons)

This is a gold crown of King James IV of Scotland and I of England. James ruled Scotland for thirty-six years before also becoming King of England and Ireland after the death of Queen Elizabeth I in 1603. The thistle on this coin, minted in London, showed the king's connection to Scotland.

It is believed that King James had relationships with men throughout his life, in particular the Duke of Buckingham, George Villiers. The king wrote a letter to George describing him as his 'wife', which has been used by many historians to suggest the relationship had a romantic element. It is also believed that James had relationships with other women outside of his marriage to Queen Anne of Denmark, such as Anne Murray who was a member of the Scottish royal court. Although many have argued he had a long line of lovers, he certainly had some affection for his wife.

Much like with other relationships at that time, the language and lack of direct sources explicitly describing events makes it difficult to say for certain the true nature of some of these relationships. A lot was also down to speculation made by attendants at court, which can often be misleading. It is likely that King James did have romantic or even sexual relations with both men and women throughout his life, but we may never know which were genuine.

A gold thistle crown coin of King James I of England and VI of Scotland, IOW-2BFC3E.

An engraving of King James with his wife, Queen Anne of Denmark, by Renold Elstrack, 1651. (Image courtesy of the Met Museum, Harris Brisbane Dick Fund, 1928. Accession number: 28.7.13)

This is a stoneware bottle dating from between 1840 and 1850. It was made for Seelie's Wine and Spirit warehouse in London and would have likely contained gin. 'Seelie's' probably refers to William Seelie who owned the Shakespeare Tavern, which may have been the same building that became the Shakespeare's Head pub in Soho, London. The original owners of the current Shakespeare's Head pub were relatives of William Shakespeare himself.

William Shakespeare, world-famous playwright, not only wrote LGBTQ+ narratives within his works, but is also believed to have had same-sex attraction himself. Although very little is known about Shakespeare, accounts of his life and references in his works have been used to point towards his romantic interest in both men and women.

There are 126 of Shakespeare's sonnets addressed to an unknown individual named the 'Fair Lord' or the 'Fair Youth' and the language within them suggests a strong romantic connection. However, many have refuted this claim and suggested that the sonnets were purely fictionalised or that the tone was that of a strong male friendship. However, there are still some who believe the words indicate Shakespeare had same-sex desires. At a time when it was illegal to have same-sex relationships, it would be unsurprising if such desires had to be hidden behind contemporary tropes of friendship or passed off as fiction.

A stoneware bottle referencing Shakespeare, SUR-2DB2B2.

This is a button depicting Queen Anne, who ruled England, Scotland and Ireland between 1702 and 1714. As a child, Anne met Sarah Jennings who was a lady-in-waiting at the court of Anne's father, King James II. Sarah would prove to be a hugely important figure in Anne's life, with the two writing to each other on a regular basis. These letters became the basis for speculation, both in the modern day and during Anne's reign, that the two might have been lovers.

The pair had secret names for one another, Anne being Mrs Morley and Sarah Mrs Freeman, which they perhaps used in their correspondence to hide their true identities. One quote from Anne, when she was a princess, was ''Tis impossible for you ever to believe how much I love you except [if] you saw my heart.' As has been mentioned elsewhere, love can be platonic and the extent of the intimacy between the two is not clear from this reading alone. However, later events in Anne's life suggest more may have happened between the two.

After the death of her husband, Queen Anne sought comfort in Abigail Hill who was a 'woman of the bedchamber', meaning she was a personal attendant to the queen. It is believed she had grown tired of Sarah, who had a very domineering temperament. Sarah wrote of the queen and Abigail's relationship, perhaps out of jealousy, suggesting there was a sexual element to it.

A silver button showing a bust of Queen Anne, LON-08B23.

When as Queen Anne of great renown
Britain's sceptre swayed
Beside the Church she dearly loved
A dirty chambermaid

O Abigail that was her name
She starched and stitched full well
But how she pierced this royal heart
No mortal man can tell

An illustration of Queen Anne and a poem written by Arthur Mainwaring, friend of Sarah Churchill, which reads: 'When as Queen Anne of great renown, Britain's sceptre swayed. Beside the church she dearly loved, a dirty chambermaid. O Abigail that was her name, she starched and stitched full well. But how she pierced this royal heart, no mortal man can tell.'

Whether there was any truth in these accusations, we are unlikely ever to know for certain. However, the sources that describe these relationships have been used to suggest more romantic associations between the queen and women at her court, influencing the production of a 2018 movie that dramatised the queen's later life.

A portrait of Sarah Churchill by Sir Godfrey Kneller. (Image courtesy of Wikimedia Commons)

Chapter 2
The Natural World

There have been many documented instances of same-sex activity within the natural world. Of course, it is difficult to understand the reasons behind these encounters as they are purely based on human observation. We are limited to understanding sex in animals based on our own practices. Similarly, biological sex has been shown to go beyond a binary in many species including humans, whether this is considering variations in genitalia, chromosomes or other factors.

It has only been in recent history, with greater numbers of openly LGBTQ+ people working in scientific fields and conducting this research, that these alternative perspectives have developed further. Previous studies would have ignored the possibility of long-term pairings between same-sex animals, which in humans we might consider as 'romantic'. This is because many believed that procreation was the key focus for sexual activity in the natural world. With more research, this is increasingly recognised as untrue.

Sexual activity within many species, especially but not limited to mammals, can be a social bonding activity or for pleasure, just as much as it can be for creating new life. The range of sexual activity varies between species as well, showing that there are many similarities with humans.

Some of the subjects in this chapter also relate to animals and plants that have become associated with individuals or groups within the LGBTQ+ community. Natural symbolism has been used throughout the past century to help reinforce the idea that being LGBTQ+ is natural and should be considered as such by all.

This object possibly shows a giraffe. It has a lot of similarities in style to the sorts of badges used to decorate caps, particularly those for people connected with the military or acting as a livery. A livery is symbol or design used to designate a particular connection to an organisation. Liveries can be a uniform or a particular emblem, often in the form of a badge. Giraffes are not found on any known livery or military badges, however, and it could be this object was used to decorate something else entirely.

Research has shown that giraffe males regularly have sexual contact with one another. Zoologist Anne Innis Dagg spent time observing giraffes in the wild and noted that, when two giraffes are spotted showing sexual behaviour, 94 per cent of the time it is two males doing so. Initially this behaviour had been interpreted by other zoologists as males trying to assert their dominance over one another. Anne's research showed that most of the time this behaviour was because the males wanted to do it and it wasn't related to power display or status.

Male-male giraffe courtship is known as 'necking'. This activity involves two male giraffes standing side by side and rubbing their necks together. Unlike the act of aggression this was originally believed to be, this behaviour is very gentle and can last up to an hour. Necking can also lead to one or both giraffes licking or sniffing the other's genitals and even 'mounting'. In some instances, males have been seen to ejaculate during this practice, adding more weight to the idea that this is intentionally sexual activity.

Above: A copper-alloy badge in the form of a Giraffe, LVPL-714DA6.

Right: A pair of male giraffes. (Image courtesy of Pexels)

This is a lead toy bear, probably dating to the 1800s and possibly from a Christmas cracker or used in a board game. Lead toys were quite common from the 1600s into the 1900s, as lead was an easy and cheap material to mass-produce things with. It wasn't until less toxic alternatives like plastic were developed that lead stopped being used as much.

Bears are a subgroup within the gay community, characterised as being larger, hairy men. Animals have been quite a popular way of differentiating different groups within the LGBTQ+ community. Other examples include skinny hairy men being called 'otters'. It is likely these subgroups were borne out of a desire to find those who were similar, both

A modern lead toy or figurine of a bear, NLM-51EE71.

physically and in terms of shared interests. This is why some groups are not just based around physical similarities but other shared traits, such as 'gaymers' who are gay men who enjoy playing video games.

The bear subculture began in the 1980s in San Francisco, with *Bear Magazine* being first published in 1987. In the early days, some bears decided to separate from the wider gay community due to intolerance and a feeling of being judged or shamed for their body type. To this day division can still be seen with some subgroups, demonstrated, for example, by the existence of bear bars and events such as bear pride, held annually in Sitges, Spain.

Above left: Photograph of Richard Bulger, founder of *Bear Magazine*, 4 July 1990. (Image courtesy of Wikimedia Commons)

Above right: A European brown bear. (Image courtesy of Pexels)

This is a copper-alloy Iron Age terret, used to connect straps in a horse harness, with ducks cast around the object. Ducks and other birds were a popular form of decoration in Iron Age metalwork. Most of these designs are considered to be ducks as they appear to imitate being on water, with the legs not visible.

Several species of duck have been known to exhibit same-sex sexual behaviour. A breeding programme for blue ducks in 2009 was abandoned because, in the group of one female and two male ducks, the males bonded with one another and ignored the female.

Studies of mallards, the most common duck species in the UK, have shown that male-male sexual activity happens in about 19 per cent of the population. This is even greater than what is believed to be the case for humans, which is often said to be 10 per cent.

It has also been observed that a female duck can turn male if it gets an injury or infection in its ovaries. Ducks' dominant sex is male, due to the Z chromosome being present in both male and female ducks. Therefore, if there is an irregularity on the part of the body associated with the W chromosome, and more importantly the production of oestrogen, the male chromosome will take over.

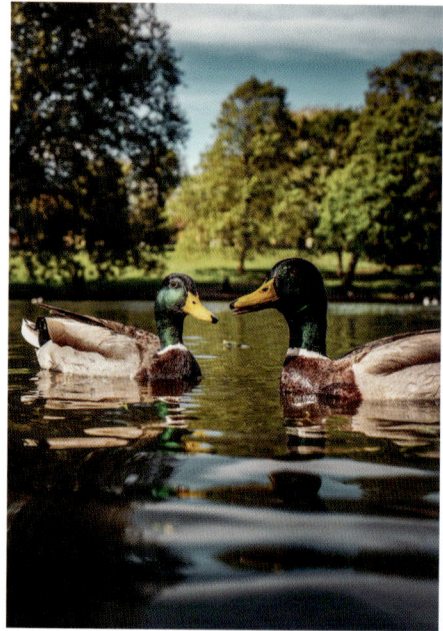

Above left: A copper-alloy Iron Age terret ring with ducks on, YORYM-C37EB7.

Above right: A pair of male mallard ducks. (Image courtesy of Pexels)

This is a copper-alloy stud in the shape of a flower, dating 1400–1700 CE. It has turned green through oxidation and would have originally been a shiny bronze colour. This would have been used to decorate a leather strap, perhaps as part of a horse harness or a belt.

The green carnation, a type of flower, has become associated with the poet and playwright Oscar Wilde. He was born in Dublin in 1854 and would become one of the most well-known writers from the Victorian era. He published many books and plays, which continue to be popular to this day.

In 1884, Oscar Wilde married Constance Lloyd and the pair had two children. Two years after their marriage, however, Wilde met Robert Ross who was seventeen years old at the time and a fan of Wilde's work. Ross was arguably Wilde's first and longest standing male relationship.

Oscar Wilde had several other notable male partners throughout his life. Most impactful was Lord Alfred Douglas, whose father brought criminal charges against Wilde in 1895. Homosexuality was illegal at this time and even a homosexual relationship 'without consummation' (i.e. having sex) could lead to a criminal conviction for 'gross indecency'. Wilde was eventually found guilty of this and spent two years in jail, initially in London but eventually being moved to Reading.

The Green Carnation was a book written by Robert Hitchens and published in 1894, one year before Wilde's criminal charges were brought to court. The book was clearly a fictionalised biography of Wilde's relationship with Lord Douglas and was used as evidence in the trial. Wilde had recently used a carnation as a publicity ploy for a play of his, which is believed to be why Hitchens gave it that title.

A copper-alloy stud in the shape of a flower, NARC-5FCD89.

Green carnations. Photograph by Andy Lee. (Image Courtesy of Pexels)

This silver penny originated in the Netherlands in around 1256–96 CE. It was issued by King Floris V and minted in Dordrecht. On the reverse there is a pansy in each quarter of the cross.

The word 'pansy' has been used as a derogatory word for gay men since the early 1900s. Flowers, such as pansies, are often socially regarded as feminine and so the association was intended to suggest femininity in a man. The use of this word as a slur is first recorded in the 1920s, to refer to effeminate men but not specifically homosexuals. It may date from earlier than this, without having been recorded. Anyone can, of course, enjoy flowers without it influencing their gender identity.

In 2005 Paul Harfleet set up 'The Pansy Project'. The focus of the project is to plant pansies at sites of homophobic abuse. It started in the UK but now has an international reach. Each pansy is recorded with its location marked on an interactive map and each is given a title that relates to the nature of the incident it records. Many of the examples include homophobic slurs and descriptions of the events that took place. Further information and the map can be found on 'The Pansy Project' website.

Above: A silver penny of King Floris V of the Netherlands, PUBLIC-55A0E4.

Right: Pansies. Photograph by Samuel Hájnik. (Image courtesy of Pexels)

This is a copper-alloy Roman figurine of a ram, a male sheep, dating to around 100–350 CE. Rams and sheep were often associated with Faunus, the god of the countryside. It is possible this figurine was from a shrine to the god, or perhaps was simply decorative within a Roman house.

Several studies have shown that rams have an 8–10 per cent chance of exclusive homosexual interaction. A further study showed that up to 20 per cent could be bisexual.

Left: A copper-alloy Roman figurine of a ram, NMS-411EC5.

Below: An illustration of NMS-411EC5.

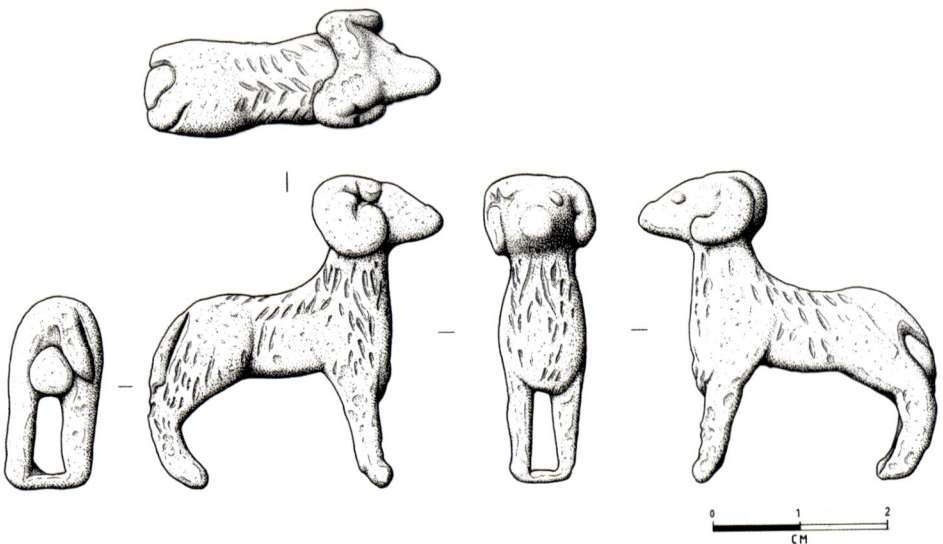

Two rams on a snowy mountain. Photograph by Irina. (Image courtesy of Pexels)

These studies observed that the behaviour was not purely sexual activity, but also involved the surrounding 'courtship' behaviours that are associated with sexual activity with females. This includes things such as nudging and making specific noises to get the attention of their partner. From a human perspective, we could perhaps consider this as 'flirting'.

Same-sex activity has been observed in female sheep, but it doesn't seem to be as common as with males. Like with other species, it was once suggested that this activity was intended to establish a hierarchy or to assert dominance between males. However, it seems clear that rams that exclusively have sexual activity with rams are no more or less dominant than those that have sex with females.

Further to this, studies have shown that 2–3 per cent of sheep are asexual, showing absolutely no interest in mating. This demonstrates that sexual reproduction, though biologically present in sheep, is not always guaranteed or desired in the species. With more and more research into animal behaviour, it is becoming clear that sex is not something wanted by every living thing.

This is part of a handle for an item of cutlery, decorated with the biblical scene of Jonah being swallowed by a whale. Dating to the 1600s, biblical scenes were often depicted on everyday items to remind Christians of important religious stories. Very few people would have seen an actual whale in the 1600s, so it is often shown as a very large fish.

In January 2022, the first ever recording of sexual activity between humpback whales was made off the coast of Hawaii. Photographers Lyle Krannichfeld and Brandi Romano spent a long time following and photographing the whales to document the event. What was not expected was that the two whales in the recording turned out to be male.

A copper-alloy handle showing Jonah inside a whale, LIN-F16D33.

Two humpback whales. Photograph by Ben Philips. It is similar to the image taken in January 2022 by Lyle Krannichfeld and Brandi Romano. The sex of the whales in this picture are unknown. (Image courtesy of Pexels)

Although most articles documenting the encounter give reasons for the activity being a display of dominance or 'practising' sexual activity, there is also a strong possibility that same-sex animal encounters simply occur for fun. Though we can never truly know about concepts such as love or relationships in animals, we do know that same-sex activity, as for humans, could also be with the intention of pleasing one or both parties.

Chapter 3
Language and Symbols

One of the greatest challenges to historians of LGBTQ+ history are the changes in language used to discuss sexuality and gender throughout time. This book focuses primarily on the English language, but similar challenges face those studying LGBTQ+ history in every language.

Not only did certain words, such as gay, lesbian or trans, not exist in certain periods of time, but the meaning of those words has also changed throughout time. In medieval Europe it was fairly common for men to express their 'love' for one another in a purely non-romantic way, yet the word was still used to mean romantic and sexual relationships, much like today. Without explicit descriptions of the nature of certain relationships in the past, we can't know for certain whether they were heterosexual or not.

In an increasingly global world, to overcome language barriers, symbols have become a common way to represent different groups within the LGBTQ+ community. Prominent examples of this are the pride flag, which can be flown on any building, and stickers of it, which can be placed in any window, letting people walking past know that it is likely a safe space for LGBTQ+ people to visit. Communicating safety, security and understanding is one of the key purposes for developing language around LGBTQ+ identity. This is why more and more terms are being used to help better identify ourselves and others. This helps many LGBTQ+ people feel safer and more comfortable with who they are.

This is a seal matrix with the inscription 'toujours gay' around the edge. It shows a cupid with a bow and arrow, holding a butterfly in its right hand. Seals like this were personal markers to sign documents by impressing the object into soft wax. Each would have been unique to the owner, business or family and would have acted as proof of authenticity.

In this instance the word gay means 'happy'. The entire phrase means 'always happy' in French. The use of the word to refer to homosexuality has only existed since the early 1900s or possibly the late 1800s. There are earlier references to the term in relation to sex work, with a 'gay house' being a brothel. Therefore a 'gay boy' was a man working in a brothel, often at the service of other men. However, its more widespread usage to refer to men who had sex with men came much later.

A glass intaglio with the words 'toujours gay' inscribed around the top, SUR-FDC7C.

THE GREAT SOCIAL EVIL.

Time:—Midnight. A Sketch not a Hundred Miles from the Haymarket.

Bella. "AH ! FANNY ! HOW LONG HAVE YOU BEEN *GAY* !"

A cartoon from *Punch* magazine published in 1857. It shows Bella asking her friend Fanny 'How long have you been gay?' referring to sex work. (Image courtesy of Wikimedia Commons)

The cupid itself and indeed the butterfly have also been used as symbols within the LGBTQ+ community. Cupid was one of the Ancient Greek 'erotes', gods of love, and has been seen as a symbol and protector of homosexual love for some time. The butterfly, although not an exclusively LGBTQ+ symbol, has been used to represent fragility and rebirth, both of which resonate with many within the LGBTQ+ community.

This is a copper-alloy object in the shape of a labrys, a double axe. The double axe has been seen in imagery as far back as the Bronze Age in the Mediterranean, used to decorate cave sanctuaries and other religious sites on Minoan Crete in the Neopalatial period, around 1700–1450 BCE. By the Roman period, the labrys had become associated with the Amazons, a group of all-female warriors who chose to live without men. The Amazons may have been entirely fictional or loosely based on a real society that existed.

The labrys became a symbol adopted by the lesbian community, probably due to its association with the Amazons and even the earlier connection with Minoan mother goddess worship. The Minoan culture on Crete has also been seen by some as a matriarchal society, with women having equal or more power than men. Therefore, some modern feminists, including many lesbians, were drawn to this culture for inspiration in their writing and artwork.

The labrys even features on one of the flags used by lesbians during Pride events. However, many lesbians today will not use this flag for two reasons. It was designed by a cisgendered gay man and many prefer to use a flag designed by a lesbian. It has also been adopted by Trans Exclusionary Radical Feminist (TERF) lesbians, and many other lesbians do not wish to be associated with them, seeking a more trans-inclusive flag instead.

A copper-alloy object in the form of a double-sided axe, known as a labrys, NARC-598D14.

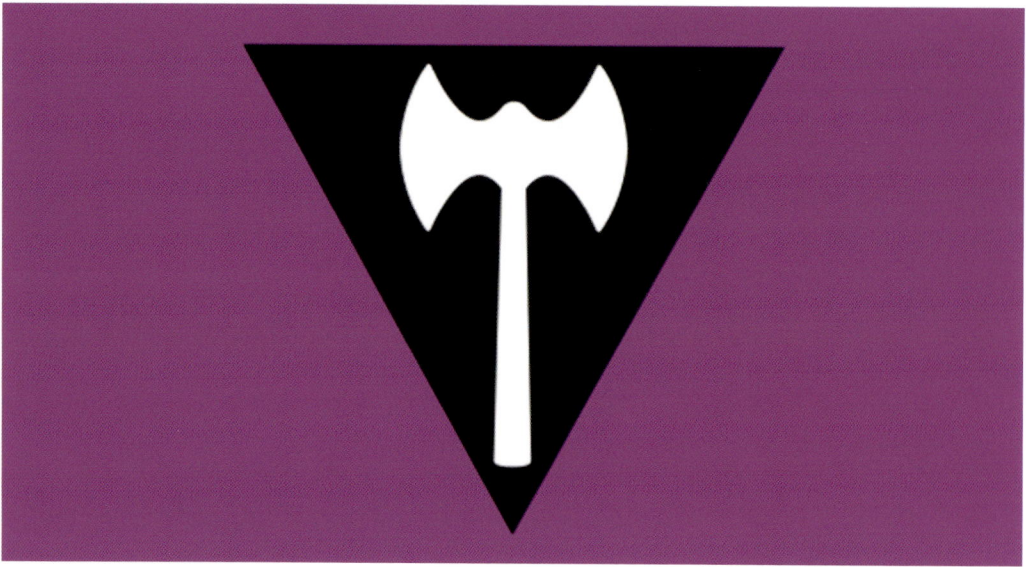

A lesbian flag containing a labrys design. (Image courtesy of Wikimedia Commons)

This is an Iron Age stater, a type of early gold coin, produced in Britain around 60–20 BCE. On one side is a horse, galloping to the right, surrounded by symbols including a double-crescent moon. On the reverse is a cross with a double-crescent moon in the centre.

The use of a pink and blue triangle to identify bisexuals was first used in 1987, having been designed by Liz Nania for the March on Washington for lesbian and gay rights. An upside-down pink triangle was worn by prisoners of concentration camps who were believed to be homosexuals or trans women in Nazi Germany and other Nazi-occupied territories. Different coloured triangles, or a yellow Star of David for Jewish people, were used for different groups to identify the reason for their imprisonment. Many gay men and trans women kept in these camps still faced prison when they were released, as the anti-homosexuality law in Germany was still in place until 1969.

A double-crescent design was later adopted by Vivian Wagner in 1998 as an alternative. This new design was sought as some bisexuals wanted to find a more unique symbol for them and many felt the use of the triangles, a symbol that caused death and harm to thousands during the 1930s and 1940s, was not appropriate.

A gold stater of Addedomarus, an Iron Age ruler of Britain in the years 25–10 BCE. One side shows back-to-back crescent moons, BH-0C605C.

This is an Iron Age horse harness fitting with a design resembling the symbol for infinity. Although the design has existed for thousands of years, its mathematical use only began in the 1600s.

In more recent years, the infinity symbol has been adopted as a sign for polyamorous people. Understandably, the concept of no end and continuity resonates with individuals who have more than one romantic or sexual partner in their life. The symbol has been incorporated into a heart design and is sometimes used on flags representing polyamorous people.

The symbol has also been adopted by individuals who identify as neurogender. These are people who believe their gender resonates more closely with their neurotype than their physical body. This means autistic or ADHD individuals may see that as a more identifying factor than their gender. In this instance, the infinity symbol represents the never-ending nature of gender in connection to neurotype, moving away from a binary seen by some.

A copper-alloy Iron Age terret fitting with an infinity symbol, LANCUM-8B4C1D.

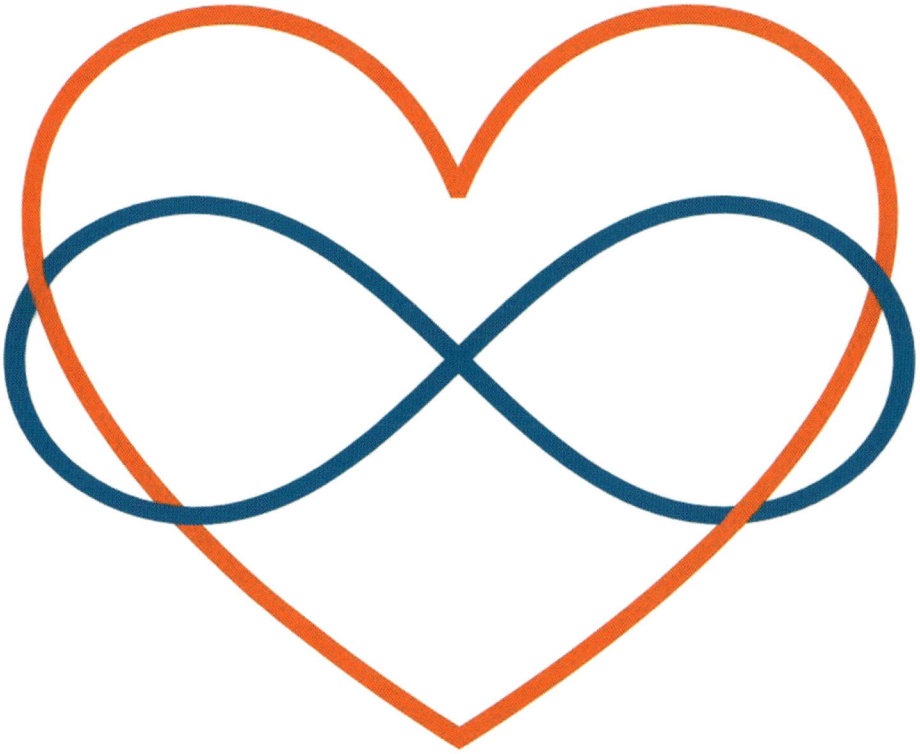

A heart with an infinity symbol, a symbol of the polyamorous community.

The neurogender flag. (Image courtesy of Wikimedia Commons)

This is a silver vinaigrette, which would have contained a strong-smelling liquid and was kept within a handkerchief to revive and invigorate the owner by sniffing it. It dates to the 1800s and has a design made from wire, known as filigree, in the form of a flower.

In some mining areas of California, especially during the Gold Rush of the mid-1800s, women were scarce. However, the men still craved entertainment and one popular activity was dancing. As most dances at the time had gendered roles, a coloured handkerchief would be used to indicate who had the male part and who had the female part.

In the 1900s this method of using handkerchiefs to identify a person's 'role' was adopted by gay men to indicate a person's sexual preference. It also spread to include specific kinks, acting as a subtle way of indicating your preferences to others with similar interests without raising the suspicions of police. Anti-Homosexuality laws weren't fully repealed in all US states until 2003, meaning secrecy within the community was reliant on symbols like these for a long time.

A vinaigrette containing scented liquid which would have been put inside a hanky, BERK-A89F87.

Los 41 maricones encontrados en un baile de la Calle de la Paz el 20 de Noviembre de 1901 by José Guadalupe Posada, 1901. (Image courtesy of the Met Museum, gift of Jean Charlot, 1930. Accession number: 30.82.107)

This is an iron Pappenheimer rapier sword, dating to the 1600s. It was found on the foreshore of the River Thames in London. This type of sword was a favourite of German and Dutch soldiers at the time but may have been owned by an English duellist if it dates from the latter end of the 1600s. Originally such swords were used on the battlefield, but rapiers like this became fashionable dress accessories for those wealthy enough to own them.

Swords like this were often used with imagery of powerful women in renaissance art. It has been suggested that depicting women with swords was meant to show their power over the penis. These women often retained their femininity, wearing typically feminine clothing and having long hair, whilst being placed in a position of power over the men in the scene or in male roles, such as a soldier.

An interest in women with swords has become popular amongst some lesbians, perhaps because of the same connotations that were first suggested in renaissance art. One of the more notable figures that has become associated with this trend is Joan of Arc. Joan was not only a warrior woman who played with gender roles, she also refused male partners throughout her life. There is no clear evidence to suggest anything of Joan's gender or sexuality, partly because she never definitively spoke of it herself. However, she was clearly an influential gender non-conforming person who has been adopted by many modern LGBTQ+ people as a symbol of liberation.

Left: An iron Pappenheimer rapier handle, LON-D29987.

Opposite above left: *Debore* by Gilles Rousselet. (Image courtesy of the Met Museum, The Elisha Whittelsey Collection, The Elisha Whittelsey Fund, 1966. Accession number: 66.559.72)

Opposite above right: A copper-alloy figurine of Joan of Arc, COLEM:1954.207. (Copyright Colchester Museums)

DEBORE Prophetiffe et Gouuernante des Hebreux, harangue deuant les Notables du
Peuple, et les prepare à la liberté et à la guerre contre les Cananeans. Li. Iudicum cap. 4.
Vignon inuent.   Abrah: Bosse et Bosse Sculpserunt.   Mariette excudit.   Cum priuilegio Regis et Regina Regenti.

49

This is a copper-alloy cockerel, probably from a pipe tamper, dating to the 1600s. As tobacco became more common in England, smoking equipment became more varied. Pipes, tobacco jars and tampers like this were often decorated in a range of designs.

Language continues to be both a powerful weapon against and a powerful tool for the LGBTQ+ community. Throughout history, words have changed their meaning and been adopted or rejected depending on changing attitudes within society. Due to this, in the 1800s and possibly earlier, gay men started to communicate with one another using a secretive and not widely used language known as Polari. Polari was developed in theatres, circuses and fish markets as a sort of short-hand language, drawing on many other languages from across the world in the process. The use of Polari by gay men was to communicate without attracting any unwanted attention at a time when being gay was illegal.

The word 'chicken' meant 'young man' in Polari and was used by gay men specifically to refer to those unfamiliar or inexperienced with homosexuality. Originally the term came from sailors, who would refer to the youngest on the ship as 'chickens'. Some have suggested the term had a more sexual connotation, too, specifically referring to young male sex workers. However, it seems the term was used, at times, more broadly than that.

Bona to vada your dolly old eek!

Part of a copper-alloy pipe tamper in the form of a chicken, NLM-D6C069.

This is a fragment of a Roman jet ring. The Romans believed jet was magical, perhaps because it was so rare or perhaps because it has electrostatic properties. Electrostatic means that, when you rub it, it causes some materials to stick to it through an electrical charge. In the same way, the Romans thought that amber was magical as it has similar properties.

Black rings have been used in recent history to identify asexual people. They are often worn on the middle finger of the right hand. The first reference to this practice can be found in 2005, on an AVEN forum on the internet, but posts suggest that the practice was already established at this time.

A black circle, when written or drawn, also denotes asexuality as well as genderless identity. The origins of this usage are harder to identify, but it is featured on the asexual flag.

To contrast with this, a white ring worn on the same finger has been used to refer to aromantic people. Aromantic people are those who feel no romantic attraction towards others, but some can still have sexual desire.

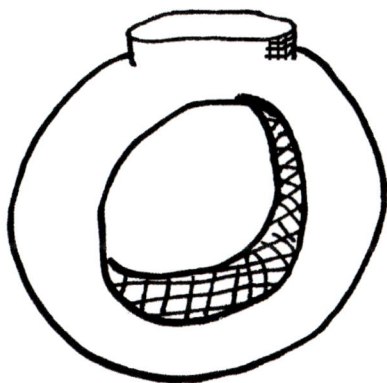

A Roman black jet finger ring – LIN-C75F03.

This is a ceramic brick, possibly made in the Netherlands, dating to the 1600s or 1700s. Although brick styles have remained fairly consistent throughout history, hardly changing in shape, size or material, there are phases when new methods were used and regions where different materials and colours became more prominent.

A white brick, probably made in the Netherlands in the 1600s or 1700s, OXON-B0F531.

On 28 June 1969, a riot started at the Stonewall Inn in New York City. Police had raided the premises in the early hours of the morning, which was a common occurrence at the time. On this occasion, due to increased tensions between the LGBTQ+ community and police as well as a growing civil rights movement across the United States, the police were met with resistance.

The resistance initially came in the form of a refusal to comply. During raids, those in the bar were asked to show a form of identification and, if they couldn't, they would be arrested. There were also dress laws in place, meaning men and women had to wear certain clothing or face arrest. Whilst waiting for police wagons to arrive to take those arrested and the alcohol away from the premises, a crowd gathered outside the building. As one woman, whose identity is believed to be Stormé DeLarverie, was arrested she started to incite the crowd to action and the riots eventually kicked off.

Although it has been long suggested that someone, either Marsha P. Johnson or Sylvia Rivera, two trans women of colour, were the first to 'throw a brick' at Stonewall, there is no consensus about whether this was the case, or even whether bricks were thrown. The riots continued the next day and one year later, the first 'gay pride' marches happened across the United States to commemorate the event.

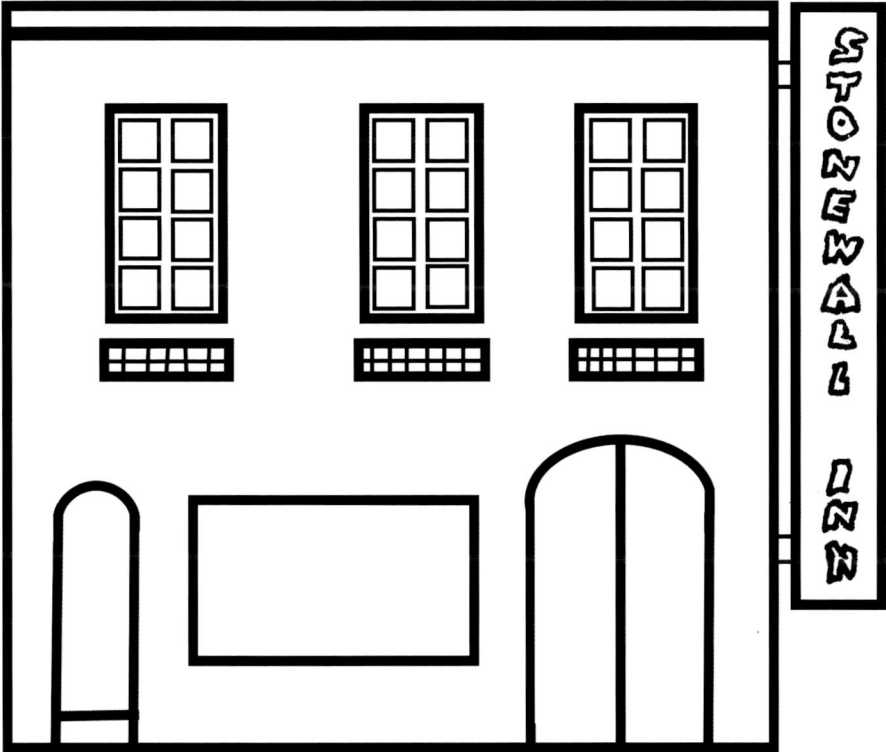

This is a hat badge depicting a sheep, probably the 'Paschal Lamb' or the 'lamb of Passover', holding a flag with the St George's Cross on it. Badges such as this were used by military personnel to show which regiment they belonged to. This one has the inscription 'The Queens' in the banner beneath it, suggesting it belonged to a member of The Queen's Royal Regiment West Surrey. The regiment was in existence from 1661 to 1959. This one is likely from sometime between 1881 and 1920, based on the material and design.

A copper-alloy badge of a lamb holding a flag of St George, SUSS-5F4661.

A more recent version of SUSS-5F4661. (Image courtesy of Wikimedia Commons)

A Pride march. Photograph by Christian Gutiérrez Martínez. (Image courtesy of Pexels)

Flags have long been used to indicate places of safety and to attract similar minded people together. Although initially there was only one 'Pride Flag', over the years different subgroups within the LGBTQ+ community have produced their own flags.

The first 'rainbow flag' to symbolise pride was created by Gilbert Baker in 1978. It was specifically for a San Francisco Gay Freedom Day celebration, produced as an alternative to the pink triangle that had been used previously. The original contained eight stripes, each representing a different quality of the LGBTQ+ community. Today, the flag has seen many changes, with variants of the 'Progress Pride' flag being a more common choice, including colours to represent trans people and people of colour.

This is a medieval seal matrix with a Roman intaglio fitted into the centre. The intaglio depicts a winged messenger, possibly Victory, saluting the god Jupiter. The inscription reads 'SECRETI NVNCIVS', which is a misspelling of '*Secreti Nuntius*', meaning 'secret messenger'. This suggests the seal may have originally been used on secret documents, not intended to be seen by anyone other than the sender and receiver.

In the centre of the intaglio are two symbols from the Greek alphabet, ν (nu) and λ (lambda). The significance of these symbols is unclear in the context of the intaglio and it was likely of little significance to the medieval user as the intaglio was produced almost 1,000 years earlier. There are several other Greek letters on the object and they might have signified the original maker or user in some way, perhaps a Greek with the letters indicating their name.

In more recent history, the letter λ is a symbol of LGBTQ+ liberation, in particular the movement from the 1960s onwards seeking equality. In 1974, the symbol was declared the international symbol of gay and lesbian equality by the Gay Rights Congress in Edinburgh, Scotland.

Sadly, the symbol has also been adopted by other groups, such as the 'white supremacist identitarian' movement. The symbol has been used less and less by the LGBTQ+ community in recent years to avoid confusion.

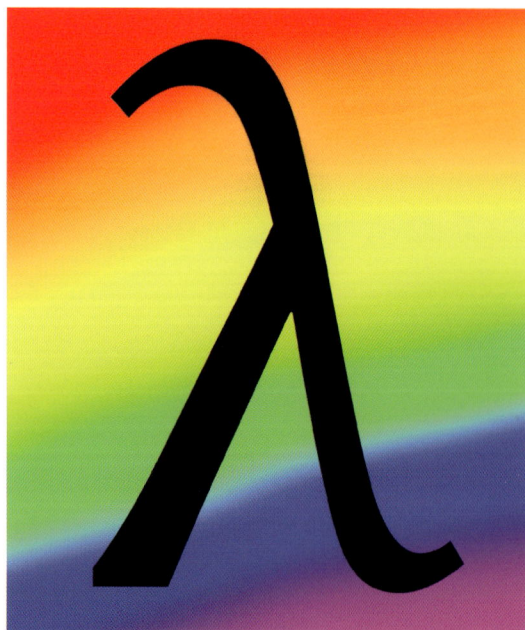

Above left: A silver medieval seal matrix containing a Roman intaglio with the letter lambda (λ) on it, YORYM-13A179.

An early medieval copper-alloy escutcheon, used to decorate a hanging bowl, dating to 600–1000 CE. It depicts a warrior with a large beard wearing a helmet. The purpose of hanging bowls is not known for certain. From other more complete examples that have been found, it is clear that rings would have attached to the rim of a bowl so it could be hung from a hook. This may have been on a wall, as a way of storing the object, or from hooks to be suspended over a fire for cooking. Escutcheons covered these rings and are often ornately decorated, as are the bowls they are attached to. This image could possibly be the Norse god Odin.

The term beard has a long history in the LGBTQ+ community to describe a woman, often a lesbian, who pretends to be the girlfriend or wife of a gay man, to help them both avoid detection in times when homosexuality was illegal. The term originates from the notion that a beard makes a face appear more masculine and that femininity, often wrongly assumed to be associated with gay men, could be hidden. The term can be seen in use as early as the 1920s, though didn't become popular until the 1960s.

A copper-alloy Anglo-Saxon escutcheon showing a bearded man, NCL-5E8820.

This is a ceramic hair or wig curler, dating to around 1650 to the 1800s. This were used to curl hair by heating it and then wrapping the hair around it. For wigs this would often be done before the wig was placed on the head.

Wigs have been a huge part of expressing gender identity throughout history. Hair length in Western society has often been used as an indicator of gender identity. For example, in recent times it was expected that women have long hair and men have short hair. However, in the 1700s long curly wigs were popular amongst men.

A ceramic wig curler dating the late 1600s to the late 1800s, PUBLIC-78CD8E.

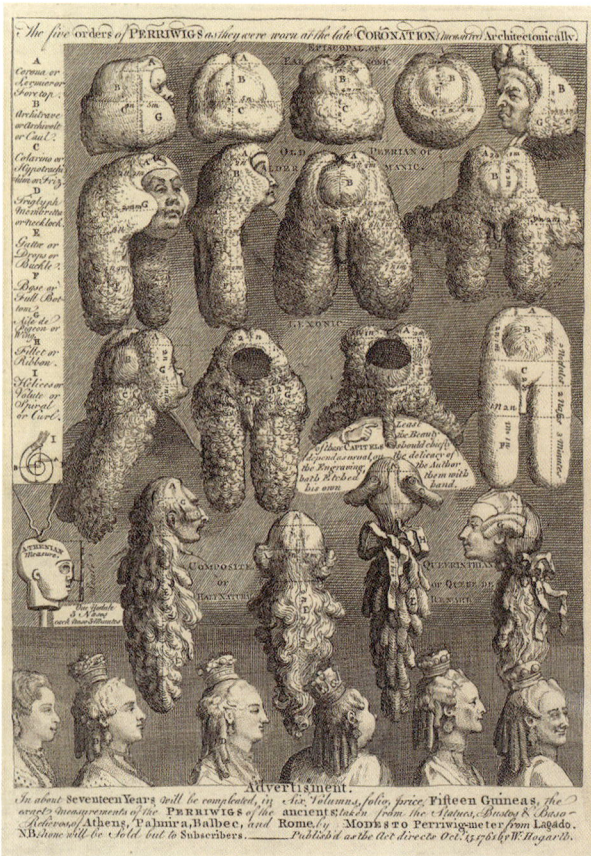

The Five Orders of Periwigs by William Hogarth, printed in 1761. (Image courtesy of the Met Museum, bequest of Phyllis Massar, 2011. Accession number: 2012.136.592)

Wigs also play an important part in drag culture, with many drag performers wearing wigs to help present the desired gender they are expressing. Sometimes these wigs are elaborate and exaggerated versions of realistic hairstyles. In more recent years, wigs are made with synthetic materials such as foam and plastic to create larger but more secure styles.

Cabinet card photograph of a man in female clothing and a wig, taken at the Pach Brothers Photography Studio in Cambridge, Massachusetts, USA, in the 1890s. (Image courtesy of Midnight Believer on Flickr)

This is a gold fede ring with a clasped hands motif and inscription on the inside, dating to the 1500s. There is what appears to be a crown or heart between the hands, suggesting this is likely from a later date. It is called a fede ring from the Italian word '*fedele*' meaning 'loyal'.

A gold finger ring with clasped hands, dating to the late 1500s, OXON-53B8DB.

The inscription on the inside reads 'MI x HART IS x YOVRS x', reading as 'My heart is yours', and is filled in with black niello. Rings with inscriptions on them are referred to as 'poesie' rings, from the French word for 'poetry'. Short phrases of affection would be inscribed on these rings as a message to a loved one. Often, these would be on the inside rather than the outside of the ring, so that the message would be a secret between the two individuals.

These were often given as wedding rings, the clasped hands representing the union of two individuals. This symbol was also common in the late 1600s, after the marriage of King Charles II and Catherine of Braganza. It has been found on countless cufflinks and buttons from this period, such as GLO-DAE729, perhaps produced and sold to commemorate their wedding.

Some might believe that same-sex couples have been given the same marriage rights as heterosexual couples within the last 100 years only. However, throughout history in many different cultures, same-sex marriage was allowed and practised. They may not have been as common as heterosexual marriages, but modern-day marriage laws are not as innovative as they may seem. Not only were several Roman emperors known to have married men, but same-sex marriages also occurred in the medieval period.

Although Christianity is often seen as primarily opposed to same-sex marriage, in the medieval period, throughout Christian Europe, same-sex marriages occurred. In Ukraine, a deacon named Evagrius supposedly went through a ceremony with a priest named Tit that was quite similar to modern weddings. Although the vows recited used the term 'brotherhood' to describe the union, every other aspect replicated a marriage, suggesting the pair were expressing a commitment to a romantic relationship.

A silver cufflink with clasped hands, dating to the late 1600s, GLO-DAE729.

Chapter 4
Mythology

Myths, legends and folklore have been used to teach morality, enforce social perspectives and entertain throughout history. Many stories have been shared across cultures and throughout time, though some elements have been added or removed depending on the attitudes of the culture sharing them.

Many mythical figures from a variety of cultures had same-sex attraction, which in some modern retellings has been lost through censorship. For example, some of the most well-known figures in Greek and Roman mythology had sexual and romantic relationships with individuals of the same sex, while others had no sexual attraction whatsoever. The fact that the original storytellers chose to include these stories, and that they were so common, suggests that it was recognised and accepted within society at the time.

In more recent times, some mythical figures and symbols have been adopted by groups within the LGBTQ+ community to represent themselves. The idea of being perceived as 'mythical' and rare, as well as some people believing we don't exist, resonates with many LGBTQ+ people.

34 and 35. Cybele and Attis
A silver denarius depicting Cybele, Kent (KENT-2769AB), and a furniture fitting depicting Attis, Shropshire (SUSS-912292)

This is a Roman denarius showing Cybele, a deity from the ancient Near East and adopted into the Roman pantheon, and a furniture fitting depicting Attis, Cybele's lover. According to mythology, Cybele was born an 'hermaphrodite', having both male and female genitals. Nowadays we would use the term 'intersex' to describe people with unclear sex or both male and female genitals. The origins of Cybele are somewhat mixed, but one story describes how the gods forced Cybele to become a woman through castration.

Cybele is often seen as a mother goddess in mythology and is believed to have origins going far back into early religions of Anatolia. There are several different versions of the myth, but most involve her relationship with a mortal named Attis. The story begins with an almond tree that grew from the spot where Cybele's discarded penis had landed. A nymph named Nana ate one of the almonds and became pregnant. She named her child Attis, but later abandoned him to be raised by a goat. One day Cybele saw Attis and, not knowing that they were sort of related, the pair immediately fell in love.

A silver denarius showing Cybele on one side, KENT-2769AB.

A copper-alloy fitting depicting a Phrygian youth, probably Attis, SUSS-912292.

A Roman figurine of Cybele on a chariot being pulled by two lions. (Image courtesy of the Met Museum, gift of Henry G. Marquand, 1897. Accession number: 97.22.24)

Alternative versions of the myth tell the story in different ways, but Attis ended up getting married to either a mortal woman or a nymph. Angered by this, Cybele turned up at the wedding and placed a curse on the entire congregation. Attis fled the wedding and castrated himself with a rock.

Priests of Cybele, known as Galli to the Romans, would castrate themselves upon entering the priesthood. We have some evidence of Galli, and thus the worship of Cybele, in Britain at sites such as Catterick. What we know about the Galli is that they were people born male but who would present as female, even outside of the religious context of the temple. They were often referred to as a middle or third gender, showing the Romans had an awareness of gender existing beyond a binary of male and female. Gender fluid or transgender identity being accepted within the context of religious life is not exclusive to the worship of Cybele and can actually be seen in many religions throughout history.

A copper-alloy mermaid, possibly dating from the Victorian period. Mermaids have long been associated with maritime folklore and legend, either as a positive or negative omen depending on the culture describing them. As a hybrid of human and fish, they are often seen as a manifestation of human desire to explore unknown worlds and liminal places. The sea, until the invention of underwater vehicles, was for that reason a mysterious symbol of the unknown.

The Little Mermaid, by Hans Christian Andersen, was itself an allegory for his unrequited love of another man, Edvard Collin, the son of Andersen's benefactor and guardian. The story reflected Andersen's real-life events. Collin revealed that he would be marrying a woman, leaving Andersen devastated. In the same way, the prince tells Ariel he will be marrying a human, leading to her taking her own life.

A copper-alloy mermaid token, NLM-6A4DC.

Above left: Hans Christian Andersen, 1873. Photograph by Thora Hallager. (Image courtesy of Wikimedia Commons)

Above right: *The Little Mermaid* sculpture, Copenhagen. Photographed by Robert Fisk. (Image courtesy of Pexels)

For centuries mermaids have also been associated with transgender identity. In Ancient Syria, the goddess Atargatis, who in one depiction has a fish's tail like a mermaid, was worshiped by a priesthood who were castrated men. Although we cannot necessarily say that those individuals were trans, they appear to have lived outside of a gender binary. In more recent history, mermaids are often seen as symbols associated with the trans community, possibly due to their ambiguous genitalia and their fluidity of living both on land and in the sea.

This is a medieval copper-alloy pendant with an enamelled design of a unicorn. These were used to decorate horse harnesses and came in a variety of shapes. This one seems to be imitating a flag or banner.

In the medieval period, unicorns were seen as symbols of virginity and death. They were often depicted alongside young virgin women in medieval art, who were believed

Above: A copper-alloy medieval harness pendant depicting a unicorn, HAMP-05D80B.

Right: The Unicorn Rests in a Garden tapestry, created between 1495 and 1505. (Image courtesy of the Met Museum, gift of John D. Rockefeller Jr, 1937. Accession number: 37.80.6)

to be the only ones who could tame them. The unicorn later became a symbol within heraldry, particularly associated with Scotland. The unicorn was believed to be a symbol of resistance to the lion, which was the heraldic animal of England.

Unicorns have been associated with the LGBT community since the early 2000s. Their rarity has also been equated with some subgroups within the LGBTQ+ community, such as bisexual polyamorous women. More specifically it was used to refer to a bisexual woman being brought into a male-female relationship as a third partner. Their association in Victorian artwork with rainbows is another possible reason for their connection with some LGBTQ+ people.

The royal coat of arms of the United Kingdom which features a unicorn, the symbol of Scotland, and a lion, the symbol of England.

An Anglo-Saxon copper-alloy object in the form of the god Woden, dating from around 600–700 CE. It is decorated with gold leaf and two small red stones, probably garnets, for eyes. Woden was the Anglo-Saxon equivalent of the Viking god Odin, who is more familiar in popular culture. It's not clear what this was once attached to, but it is likely a decorative mount for a casket or stirrups.

Some interpretations of the mythology of Woden have suggested that it was believed he did not conform to gender binaries and may even have been attracted to both men and women. In accounts, he is described as skilled in seiðr, which was women's magic according to Scandinavian mythology. He uses this feminine magic to cross boundaries, like journeying into the underworld. This use of magic specifically associated with women has led some modern historians to suggest the Anglo-Saxon people saw him as gender fluid.

A copper-alloy Anglo-Saxon depiction of Woden, BERK-DB4E15.

A depiction of Odin by Carl Emil Doepler, made in 1882. (Image courtesy of Wikimedia Commons)

For the Anglo-Saxons and Vikings, accusing a man of practising seiðr was also seen as the equivalent to accusing a man of taking the passive role in sex. This may have been the intention with Woden, which would suggest that some believed he had same-sex attraction. Though this could equally have been an attempt to make fun of the god, this would be unusual as Woden was well respected in Norse religion. Although many other accounts suggest homosexuality was punished within the Anglo-Saxon and Viking worlds, these are specifically from times when those cultures had been heavily influenced by Christianity. It is possible that earlier in the past when these myths were first created, there was a greater acceptance of same-sex desire and people who did not conform to a gender binary.

39 and 40. Mars and Venus

A Roman figurine of Mars, Surrey (SUR-1C1A4E), and a Roman figurine of Venus, Kent (KENT-E80066)

These two figurines show the Roman gods Mars, the god of war, and Venus, the goddess of love. They have long been used as symbols of masculinity and femininity, despite the images of Mars and Venus having changed throughout classical antiquity and into the modern era. The images here are the Roman versions of the gods. Mars is a symbol of masculinity, covered in armour and ready for war. Venus, the symbol of femininity, is completely naked with a slender body and long hair.

Both gods have planets within our solar system named after them. In the medieval period, the planets were given symbols to indicate them without writing their full name. The symbol chosen for Mars was a spear and shield ♂ and the symbol for Venus was a round stomach and cross marking the vulva ♀.

Above left: A copper-alloy Roman figurine of Mars, SUR-1C1A4E.

Above right: A copper-alloy Roman figurine of Venus, KENT-E80066.

Above: A symbol used by some to indicate transgender identity.

Left: *Mars and Venus United by Love* by Paolo Veronese (aka Paolo Caliari), dating to the 1570s. (Image courtesy of the Met Museum, John Stewart Kennedy Fund, 1910. Accession Number: 10.189)

The symbols of Mars and Venus were first used to refer to gender by Carl Linnaeus, a Swedish scientist, in the 1700s. His work primarily focused on plants and categorising the natural world into groups. The symbols have been merged in recent years to represent transgender individuals, or a combination of two male symbols and two female symbols to identify gay and lesbian people, respectively.

This is an early medieval stirrup mount, dating to 1000–1100 CE. These decorative plaques were applied to the outside of stirrups, used in horse riding. This particular example seems to depict a male figure in the centre with two entwined serpents running around the outside of the design. This suggests the individual could be Loki, the Norse god of mischief.

At the time this object was made much of the Scandinavian world had converted to Christianity with symbols of paganism like this being banned throughout much of Europe. These designs found in such a late context could suggest the wearers might have been continuing their pagan faith in secret or were Vikings who had not converted. They could equally be heirlooms or simply chosen for their design.

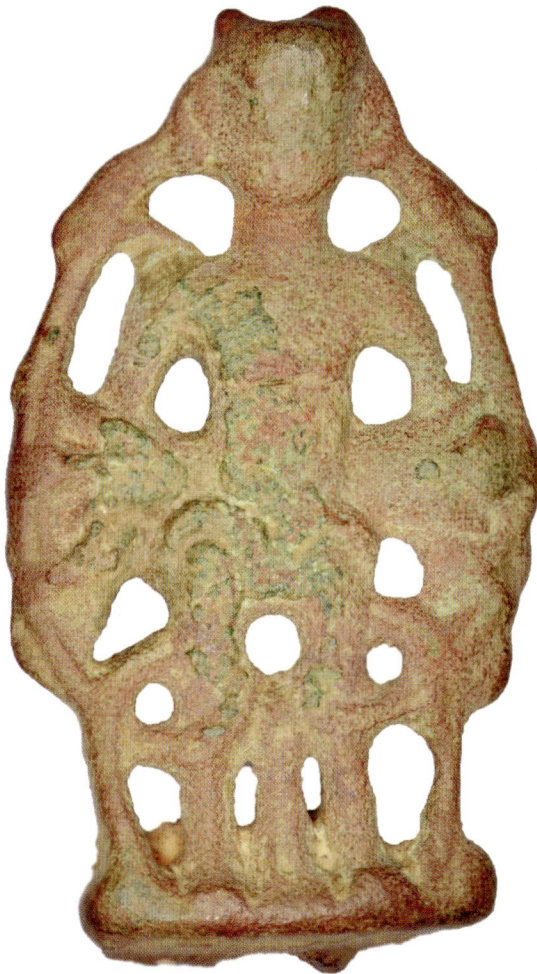

A copper-alloy stirrup mount depicting a figure with entwined serpents, SF-77A266.

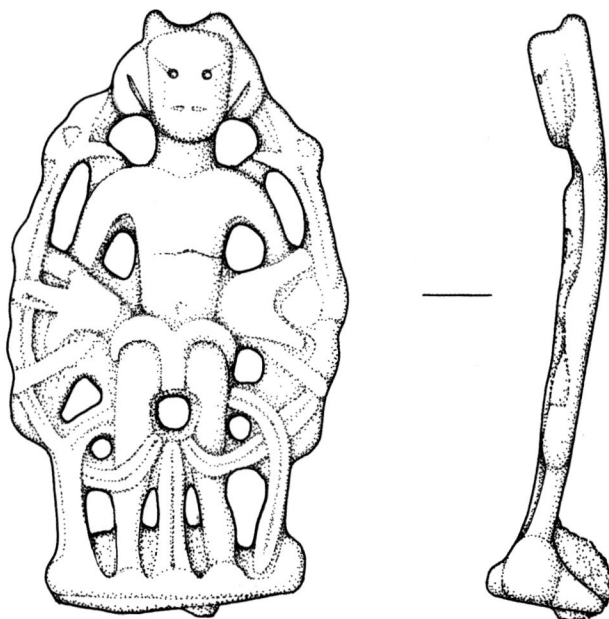

An illustration of SF-77A266.

In Norse mythology, Loki was believed to have had the power of shapeshifting. Most often he would turn into both men and women to trick others into doing what he wanted. Loki also had sex with many people, male and female, in the disguise of someone else. In the stories he seems very comfortable being a woman, making him a popular symbol with modern gender fluid and transgender people.

This is a copper-alloy figurine of the Roman god Mercury. He is wearing a winged hat, known as a *petasos*, and has a cloak that is draped over his left arm. There are traces of something in his right hand, which was likely a caduceus, a rod with snakes wrapped around it. Mercury was a god with many titles. He was primarily the god of travellers and acted as a messenger between the other gods and between the gods and mortals. He also had many similarities with the Greek god Hermes, but they were distinct individuals in mythology.

Mercury, like many Roman gods, had romantic and sexual relationships with both men and women. In one myth he accidentally killed his lover, a young man named Crocus, in a

A copper-alloy figurine of Mercury, BH-B33B24.

75

Crocus flowers.
(Image courtesy
of Pixabay,
via Pexels)

discus-throwing accident. It was believed that a crocus plant grew from where the man's blood fell and was named after him. Another notable lover was Pollux, one of the Dioscuri who were the twin brothers of the famous Helen of Troy.

The name of course is also connected to one of the greatest icons of rock music of the twentieth century. Freddie Mercury, born Farrokh Bulsara, supposedly chose the name Mercury as he was inspired by the Roman god. Freddie had to hide his sexuality at a time when it was not as accepted to be openly attracted to the same sex. Having had relationships with men and women, his sexuality is still often debated, but he has become an LGBTQ+ icon regardless.

Above left: A copper-alloy sculpture of Mercury found near Gosbecks, Colchester, COLEM:1948.2. (Copyright Colchester Museums, image credit Douglas Atfield)

This is a small figurine of Joan the Wad, a figure in Cornish folklore believed to lead lost travellers astray alongside her companion Jack O'Lantern. Figurines like this were made to bring good luck to anyone who carried them whilst travelling. In folklore, Joan is queen of the piskies, a type of Cornish fairy that are renowned for causing mischief.

The term 'fairy' has a long history with the LGBTQ+ community, specifically with gay men. The word has been used throughout history as a slur, seemingly connected to the inaccurate perception that gay men are effeminate and that fairies are more commonly associated with girls. It had its prominence as an offensive term throughout the 1900s and has since decreased in use. However, some within the LGBTQ+ community have chosen to hold on to this word and use it themselves, as has been done with several terms throughout history.

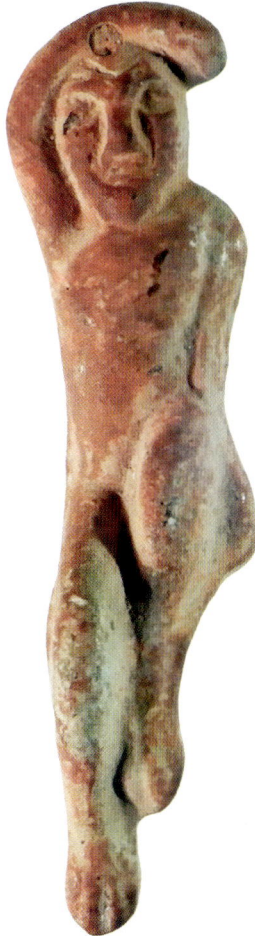

A copper-alloy figurine of the fairy Joan the Wad, NLM-830C57.

Above: Take the Fair Face of Woman, and Gently Suspending, With Butterflies, Flowers, and Jewels Attending, Thus Your Fairy is Made of Most Beautiful Things by Sophie Gengembre Anderson, painted some time before 1903. (Image courtesy of Wikimedia Commons)

Left: The Fairy Queen Takes an Airy Drive in a Light Carriage, a Twelve-in-hand, drawn by Thoroughbred Butterflies after Richard Doyle, engraved and printed in colour by Edmund Evans and published by Longman, Green, Reader and Dyer in 1870. (Image courtesy of the Met Museum, gift of Lincoln Kirstein, 1970. Accession number: 1970.565.74(13))

Fairies also have associations with Peter Pan, the eponymous character in J. M. Barrie's play. Besides the fairy character of Tinkerbell, Peter uses fairy magic to fly and stay young forever. In some of the early plays, Peter would be played by a woman, a practice that continues in British pantomimes to this day. Gender-swapping roles have a long history in theatre, partly stemming from women not being allowed to perform so men had to take female roles in plays. That was then flipped in more recent history.

Chapter 5
Communities

While in some times and places same-sex attraction and not conforming to a gender binary were more accepted, there were still many periods of history in which LGBTQ+ people were met with persecution and even death. In fact, to this day there are parts of the world where it is illegal to have same-sex relationships or to not conform to gender rules within that society. Some places still have the death penalty for those accused.

In response to this persecution, communities have formed to help protect and support those who did not feel safe. This was sometimes in secret or in some instances publicly. Some groups already existed and attracted those who were already living on the fringes of society, while other groups were formed specifically to provide safe spaces for LGBTQ+ people.

To this day, many LGBTQ+ people choose to remain within communities that are separate from wider society, to feel safe and be around similar people. Although great progress has been made within some countries, hatred of the LGBTQ+ community continues and those who have experienced that hatred deserve safe spaces to exist in.

This is an 8 ryal coin, also known as a peso. It has a connection to piracy, more through its references in popular culture than in historical reality. Throughout the 1600s, Spanish coins became a global currency due to so many having been minted. Many nations other than Spain also used them, once they had been stamped by local officials to confirm their value.

Although very few pirates had these coins pass through their hands, reference to 'Pieces of Eight' in the novel *Treasure Island* has ensured the strong associations between the coinage and the pirate world.

There are several accounts of pirates having same-sex relationships, to the extent that a form of pirate marriage was even created in response. Through this specific union, known as matelotage, pirates would form a bond with their partner to ensure that any of their possessions would pass to them when they died. These pairs were known as 'matelots' (pronounced 'ma-te-low') and later this became 'mateys', a term still used widely in depictions of pirates, though having lost its romantic meaning.

One notable example of a same-sex relationship between pirates was that of John Swann and Robert Culliford. They were recorded as living together on Ile St Marie, near Madagascar, in 1699. Swann was described as Culliford's consort, a term that traditionally refers to the partner of a monarch or a ship sailing in partnership with another. It has been assumed this term was intended to describe a romantic relationship between the two. Even Edward Teach, the infamous pirate known as Blackbeard, was believed to have had at least one same-sex relationship.

There were also many female pirates, who disguised themselves as men to get onto ships. Two notable examples were Anne Bonny and Mary Read, who were aboard the ship

A silver 8 ryal coin, DEV-AB49A5.

of (Calico) Jack Rackham. Each dressed as men to be able to get onto Jack's ship, neither knowing the other was a woman. The revelation came when Anne became attracted to Mary and felt the need to share her true identity, at which point Mary revealed she was also a woman.

Right: An engraving of Edward Teach, aka Blackbeard, made by Joseph Nicholls in 1736. (Image courtesy of Wikimedia Commons)

Below left: Anne Bonny, *Firing Upon the Crew* from the Pirates of the Spanish Main series of cards (N19), produced by George S. Harris & Sons and published by Allen & Ginter Cigarettes in 1888. (Image Courtesy of the Met Museum, The Jefferson R. Burdick Collection, gift of Jefferson R. Burdick. Accession number: 63.350.201.19.32)

Below right: Mary Read, *The Duel* from the Pirates of the Spanish Main series of cards (N19), produced by George S. Harris & Sons and published by Allen & Ginter Cigarettes in 1888. (Image Courtesy of the Met Museum, The Jefferson R. Burdick Collection, gift of Jefferson R. Burdick. Accession number: 63.350.201.19.35)

A copper-alloy mount depicting a knight in combat or at prayer. Knights were an important part of the feudal system in medieval England, acting as both law enforcement and representatives of the nobility. Being a knight was originally a military title, primarily given to those who fought on horseback. The title later led to greater wealth, power and prestige.

Accounts from the medieval period tell us that knights had romantic relationships with one another. Accusations of sodomy were brought against the Knights Templar in the 1300s and, although many of the allegations were likely attempts to weaken the power the order had in Europe, some of the accusations were probably based on truth.

A copper-alloy plaque depicting a knight in prayer, SF-DC1271.

An ornamental plaque of a knight on horseback, *c.* 1300. (Image courtesy of the Met Museums, Bashford Dean Memorial Collection, Funds from various donors, 1929. Accession number: 29.158.735)

One issue we have with understanding same-sex relationships in the past is the language that was used at the time. Words such as 'brotherhood' were used by contemporaries to describe strong male-male relationships between knights, which to us does not indicate romance but may have done at the time. The existence of liturgies (religious guidance) for bonding ceremonies that took place between knights suggest that their relationships could have been deeper. The ceremonies included hand binding and a kiss at the end, much like heterosexual marriages.

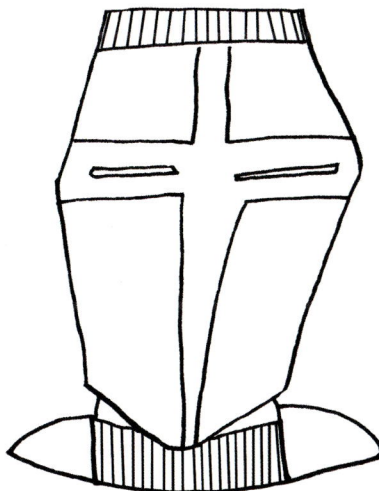

This is a token for a coffee house in London, dating to 1671. Tokens like these were produced at a time when there was not much small currency, such as pennies, in circulation. They acted as tokens to be traded for goods or services instead of coins. Coffee houses, like the one in Friday Street that issued this token, were a very new phenomenon in Britain. When this token was issued, coffee had only been introduced to the general public in the mid-1600s.

In the 1700s onwards, some coffeehouses and taverns acted as safe spaces for homosexual men wishing to meet others. At this time, the Buggery Act of 1535 made it illegal to engage in any sexual act that did not lead to having a child. Therefore, safe spaces like this were the only way to ensure men seeking sex with other men could meet without suspicion. However, they weren't completely safe as there were often raids on these properties with those in attendance and the owner of the property being arrested.

Many of these establishments were called 'molly houses'. The term molly is believed to come from the word 'moll', which meant a lower-class woman or prostitute. This probably derives from Mary, specifically referring to Mary Magdalene who was one of Jesus' followers. It was also used to refer to effeminate men, often but not always homosexuals.

A copper-alloy trade token for Andrew Vincent Coffee House in London, SUR-7BEB19.

Men Dancing in a Coffee House by Charles Grignion, after Thomas Rowlandson, from Tobias Smollett's *The Expedition of Humphry Clinker*, Vol. 1, published 1 February 1793 by James Sibbald. (Image courtesy of the Met Museum, The Elisha Whittelsey Collection, The Elisha Whittelsey Fund, 1959. Accession number: 59.533.562(2))

This is a lead pilgrim badge in the form of Thomas Becket, Archbishop of Canterbury and Christian martyr. It was produced in the 1300s and would have been bought from one of his shrines. The fact it was found in Oxfordshire does not mean that it was necessarily from a local shrine, as many people travelled far and wide on pilgrimages to the shrines of various saints that covered the Christian world. Some people even intentionally left their pilgrim badges as offerings in rivers or at other sites across the country. Hundreds of pilgrim badges have been found in the River Thames in London, suggesting this was a place where pilgrims regularly offered their badges.

Throughout much of its history, the Christian Church has openly been opposed to same-sex relationships and those who did not conform to the gender standards of the time. However, in the early days of the Church, this was not always the case.

A lead-alloy pilgrim badge of Thomas Becket, OXON-4CCCF9.

A painting depicting Alcuin of York (centre), made by Fulda. (Image courtesy of Wikimedia Commons)

In the late 700s, Alcuin of York, who was the abbot of Aachen, sent a letter to the bishop of Salzburg asking him to 'precibus rape me', which translates as 'take me with your prayers'. This phrasing has been compared to the Greek myth of Zeus and Ganymede, in which Zeus kidnapped the youth and took him to Mount Olympus to be his 'cup bearer'. Other letters written by Alcuin seem to indicate he may have had strong romantic feelings for other men as well.

48. Nuns
A badge depicting a nun, Lincolnshire (NLM-6B44E4)

This is a relatively modern copper-alloy badge, probably dating to the early 1900s. It depicts a nun in a habit, lifting the hem of the robe to reveal most of her leg. The quality of the metal and the style of depiction suggest the more recent date. One suggestion of its use is that it may have been attached to the front grille of a car, like early AA badges.

Although they have often been seen as symbols of purity and chastity, nuns throughout history have not always been celibate and some even engaged in same-sex activity. An account of Italian Mother Superior Benedetta Carlini, dating to the early 1600s, indicates that she had sex with another nun, Sister Bartolomea Crivelli. However, Bartolomea denied she was a willing participant, meaning this was more likely a case of sexual abuse. When accused of this, Sister Benedetta claimed it was the angel Splenditello acting through her that caused her to pursue a sexual relationship with Sister Bartolomea.

A copper-alloy badge of a nun, NLM-6B44E4.

Nuns at Work by Alessandro Magnasco, dating to the 1700s. (Image courtesy of the Met Museum, The Jack and Belle Linsky Collection, 1982. Accession number: 1982.60.13)

Several other accounts suggest that romantic feelings existed between nuns throughout the medieval period and later. Once again, the use of language makes it difficult to distinguish which of these relationships had deeper meanings to them. However, it is clear that many women who had taken holy orders and joined a convent would have sexual and romantic relationships with one another.

This is a medieval pendant used to decorate a horse harness. It depicts an image of 'the peacock in his pride', which was a term referring to a peacock with its tail fully displayed. It symbolised many things, including beauty, power and knowledge.

Pride has been a term used by the LGBTQ+ community to express happiness and joy in being who they are for a long time. In fact, annual celebrations of the community often have the word 'Pride' in the title. Once a single movement, championing equal rights across the world, Pride eventually became localised with many towns and cities hosting their own pride events each year.

The first 'Gay Pride March' happened on the one-year anniversary of the Stonewall riots. Although it was called the Christopher Street Liberation Day March, it became a regular occurrence that was generally called the 'Gay Pride March' and spread worldwide.

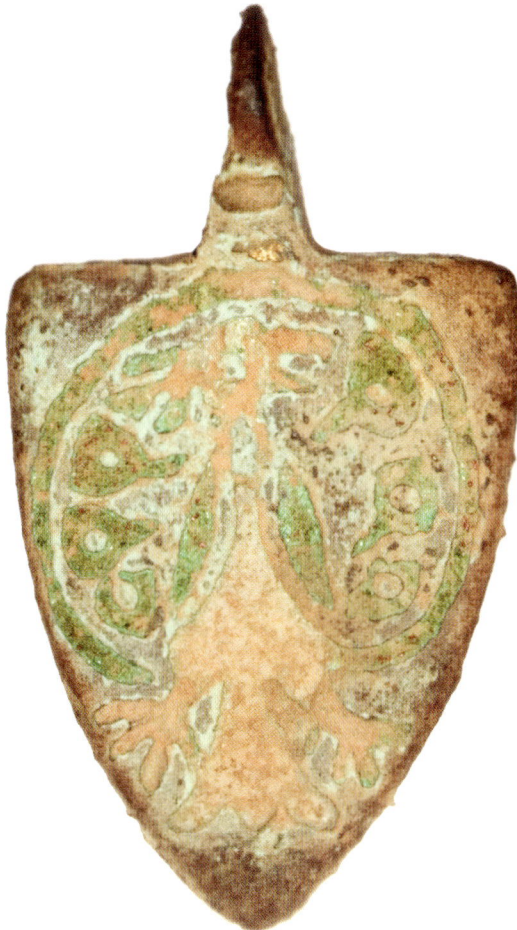

A copper-alloy harness pendant showing a 'peacock in his pride', SOM-8A2927.

Above: A banner from the 2018 'Pride in London' event held in London, Ontario, Canada. (Image courtesy of Pexels)

Left: *L'Orgueil* (*Pride*), from *Les Péchées Capitaux* (*The Deadly Sins*) by Jacques Callot. For many centuries pride, known as 'Superbia' in Latin, had a negative connotation in the Christian world, but has become a far more positive trait in recent years. (Image courtesy of the Met Museum, Bequest of Edwin De T. Bechtel, 1957. Accession number: 57.650.390(2))

Pride events tend to take place in June, which is when the Stonewall riots began. However, to try and avoid conflicts in nearby towns, these events are often spread throughout the summer in more recent years. Added to other commemorative time periods, such as LGBTQ+ History Month, which is February in the UK, there are opportunities throughout the year to celebrate progress that has been made in civil rights, whilst continuing to fight for the rights of those unable to across the world.

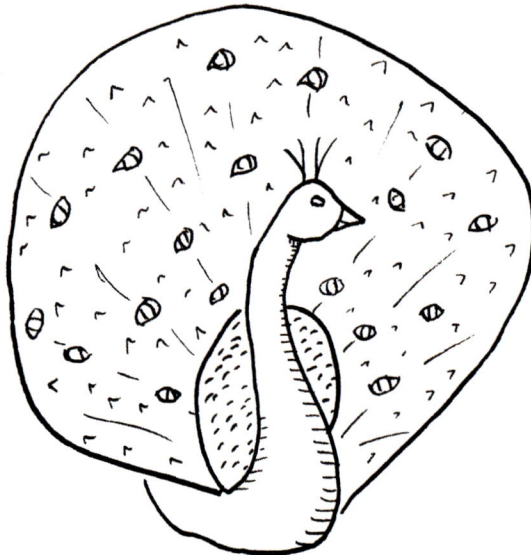

This is a copper-alloy vessel mount in the form of a reclining figure. They are almost nude, apart from a cloth draped around the waist, possibly a toga. The head, one hand and the legs are missing, though enough remains to give a sense of the pose and identify the individual as male.

The figure is likely part of a symposium scene. Symposia were Ancient Greek gatherings, usually after a large meal, where men would gather to drink and discuss a variety of subjects. The Romans had similar events known as *comissatio* or *convivium*, which followed a very similar format.

There are several symposium scenes that have been found painted on drinking vessels from Ancient Greece that show male-male flirting and sex. Further to this are countless drinking vessels that show men having sex with one another, suggesting this was often a subject of conversation (or activity) at drinking parties such as the symposia. Roman vessels have been found with similar scenes, such as the Warren Cup, though these are not as common.

A copper-alloy figurine of a male figure lying on a couch, SF-B079B1.

The underneath of a ceramic kylix, drinking vessel, dating from 480–470 BCE. The decoration shows an erastes and ermomenos at a symposium. (Image courtesy of the Met Museum, Purchase by subscription, 1896. Accession number: 96.18.143)

At the symposium male-male relationships were developed, particularly along the Ancient Greek pairing of 'erastes' and 'eromenos'. The erastes was the older man in a pair and an eromenos was the younger, sometimes with a considerable age gap. It is believed that this dynamic was established to develop the younger male and teach them the ways of the world, which in many instances included sex. Alongside these pairings at the symposia might have been a number of 'pornoi', male prostitutes who were paid for their services.

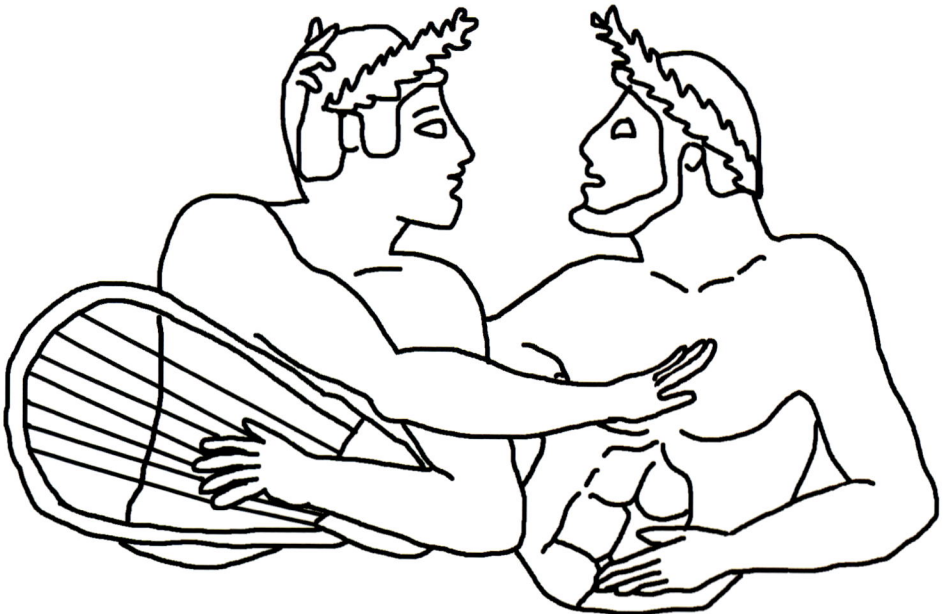

Glossary

Note: Many of these definitions change with greater awareness and understanding and aren't necessarily agreed by all.

Asexual	Someone with no sexual attraction to other people.
Aromantic	Someone with no romantic attraction to other people.
Bisexual	Someone who is attracted to men and women.
Drag	A performance art in which the gender of the performer is reversed or questioned through their appearance or actions.
Gay	A man who is attracted to other men.
Gender identity	The categorisation of a person based on social criteria of masculine and feminine.
Gender fluid	Someone whose gender identity can change throughout their lifetime or even throughout the day.
Hermaphrodite	An outdated term for an intersex individual born with both male and female genitals.
Heterosexual	Someone who is attracted to someone of the opposite sex.
Homosexual	Someone who is attracted to someone of their own sex.
Intersexed person/intersex	Someone who has biological criteria meaning they don't fit exclusively in either the male of female category. This can be due to chromosomes or genitalia.
Lesbian	A woman who is attracted to other women.
LGBTQ+	Lesbian, Gay, Bisexual, Transgender and Queer. The Q is sometimes interchanged with 'questioning' and other letters are sometimes included.
Outing	Sharing someone's sexuality or gender identity without their consent or before they are ready to share it themselves.
Pansexual	Someone attracted to individuals regardless of their gender.
Same-sex attraction	Someone who is attracted to someone of the same sex. This includes homosexual, bisexual and pansexual people.

Sex	The biological categorisation of an individual based on factors such as chromosomes and genitals.
Sexuality	A person's sexual attraction to others.
Trans/transgender	Someone whose gender identity does not correspond to the sex they were assigned at birth.
Queer	A term used to refer to a range of sexualities and gender identities. Once used as an offensive term, and still considered to be by some, it has been reclaimed in recent years by the LGBTQ+ community.

Bibliography

General

Parkinson, R. B., *A Little Gay History: Desire and Diversity Across the World*, United Kingdom: Columbia University Press, 2013

DK, *The LGBTQ+ History Book: Big Ideas Simply Explained*, London: DK, 2023

Introduction

Arnold, B., 'Intersectionality and elite identity in Iron Age west-central European mortuary contexts', in P. Brun, B. Chaume and F. Sacchetti (eds), *Vix et le phénomène princier*, Bordeaux: Ausonius Éditions

Chase, M. and M. Kowaleski (eds), *Reading and Writing in Medieval England: Essays in Honour of Mary C. Erler*, Woodbridge: Boydell & Brewer, 2019

White, T., *Experiencing Medieval Literature*, British Library, 2018 [online]

Chapter 1

Cripps, T., *William II (Rufus)*, History UK [online]

Doble, F., *Saint Sebastian as a gay icon*, ArtUK, 2020 [online]

Fox, R. L., *Alexander the Great*, London: Penguin, 1974

Fraser, A., *King James VI of Scotland, I of England*, London: Weidenfeld & Nicolson, 1975

Kittredge, C., *Francis of Assisi: queer side revealed for saint who loved creation, peace and the poor*, QSPirit, 2018 [online]

Lindon, L., *Virginia Woolf's (not so) secret lesbian relationship – in her own words*, Penguin, 2021 [online]

Seymour, P., *Edward II*, London: Yale University Press, 2011

Chapter 2

Bagemihl, B., *Biological Exuberance: Animal Homosexuality and Natural Diversity*, New York City: St Martin's Press, 1999

Burton, T. I., *Self-Made: Creating Our Identities from Da Vinci to the Kardashians*, New York City: PublicAffairs, 2023

Harfleet, P., The Pansy Project – thepansyproject.com

Rayner, E., W. Hamra and W. Shipton, 'Sexual Dimorphism and Sex Reversal in Birds', *Journal of Applied Animal Science*, 8 (3) (2015): 27–34

Roselli, C. E., R. C. Reddy and K. R. Kaufman, 'The development of male-oriented behavior in rams', *Front. Neuroendocrinol*, 32 (2) (2011): 164–69

Westphal, Sylvia Pagán, 'Glad to be asexual', *New Scientist*, 2004

Chapter 3

Baker, P., *Polari: The Lost Language of Gay Men*, London: Routledge, 2003

Carter, D., *Stonewall: The Riots that Sparked the Gay Revolution*, New York City: St Martin's Press, 2004

Deshler, K., *On Sword Lesbians*, kiradeshler.substack.com/p/on-sword-lesbians, 2021

Haysom, M., 'The double-axe: A contextual approach to the understanding of a cretan symbol in the neopalatial period', *Oxford Journal of Archaeology*, 29(1) (2010): 35–55

Heger, H., *The men with the pink triangle*, Boston: Alyson Publications, 1980

Williams, C. A., *Roman Homosexuality*, Oxford: Oxford University Press, 2009

Chapter 4

Coward, S., *Queer as Folklore*, London: Unbound, 2024

Pinto, R. and L. Pinto, 'Transgendered Archaeology: The Galli and The Catterick 'Transvestite', in *TRAC 2012: Proceedings of the Twenty-Second Annual Theoretical Roman Archaeology Conference*, Frankfurt, 2012, 169–81

Roscoe, W., 'Priests of the goddess: Gender transgression in ancient religion', *History of Religions*, 35(3) (1996), 195–230

Solli, B., 'Queering the Cosmology of the Vikings: A Queer Analysis of the Cult of Odin and Holy White Stones', *Journal of Homosexuality*, Vol. 54 (1/2) (2008), 192–208

Chapter 5

Boswell, J., *Christianity, Social Tolerance, and Homosexuality: Gay People in Western Europe from the Beginning of the Christian Era to the Fourteenth Century*, Chicago: University of Chicago Press, 2015

Burg, B. R., *Sodomy and the Pirate Tradition: English Sea-Rovers in the Seventeenth Century Caribbean*, New York City: NYU Press, 1995

Clark, D., *Between Medieval Men: Male Friendship and Desire in Early Medieval English Literature*, Oxford: Oxford University Press, 2009

Norton, R. (ed.), *Homosexuality in Eighteenth-Century England: A Sourcebook*, Rictor Norton, 2023 [online]